Why
Still
Dance

Why Still Dance

by

Phebe Hanson

Nodin Press

Acknowledgements:

"Cinderella" was first published in *25 Minnesota Poets # 2* (Nodin Press, 1977).
"Sturdy Arms" was first published in Minnesota Poetry Calendar 2001.
"Santa Lucia" and "I Listen To The Radio In Montevideo, Minnesota,
And Think Of My Son Who Will Soon Be Thirty" were first published in
Minnesota Writes: Poetry (Milkweed Editions/Nodin Press, 1987).
"Nursing" and "Meat" were first published in *Woman Poet: the Midwest*
(Women-in-Literature Inc. 1985).
"Close Call" was first published in *To Fathers: What I've Never Said* (Constance
Warloe, ed. Story Line Press, Ashland, Oregon, 2001).
"After Seeing Night and Fog" was first published in *Water-Stone* (Volume 5,
No. 1, 2002).
"Sacred Heart, Minnesota," "Grandma X," and "Still Writing, Still Painting"
were first published in *Water-Stone*, (December 2003.)
"Cottonwoods" in *Landscape of Ghosts* by Bill Holm and Bob Firth 1993
Voyager Press

Thanks to Rebecca Alm and Kathleen Heideman for the handbound limited
edition of these poems. Thanks to Marly Rusoff for finding the perfect home
for this book with Norton Stillman at Nodin Press. Thanks to Patricia Hampl,
Jill Breckenridge, Beverly Rollwagen, Carol Connolly, Pamela Holt, Bonita
Wahl, Bill Holm, Howard and Jody Mohr and countless other friends for their
years of encouragement. Thanks to Linda Gammell for her beautiful cover
photograph and to my son Erik Riese for his fine author portrait.

ISBN-1-932472-05-3

Nodin Press in a division of Micawber's, Inc.
530 N Third Street, Suite 120
Minneapolis, MN 55401

First Edition

To my children Erik, Rolf, Leah,
their spouses Mary and Ann,
and to my grandchildren
Caitlin, Emma, Woody, Kate, Lis,
Alex, Jacob, Joseph, and Linnea

Introduction

I met Phebe one evening in Morris, Minnesota, circa 1974, at a mass poetry reading called into being by Robert Bly. He was following through on his notion that the world needed a huge anthology of poems written for and about every county in Minnesota. As commandant, Robert would take his pointer and touch a county on the large map behind him and poets would rise and read. It was looking like a very long night to me until Phebe Hanson stood and read a poem about her hometown of Sacred Heart, Minnesota, which is in Renville County, if you must know. And there it was, that lively conversational voice of hers, that open honesty. And more than that, as I told her when I went over to shake her hand, she was darn funny. It's the only poem I remember from that night. She was 46 years old and new at the poetry game. She got a late start, but she caught up fast.

I have heard Phebe read her poems many times since that night, sometimes before a large audience, and sometimes when she visited us on the prairies of southwestern Minnesota, near Cottonwood, in Lyon County. Phebe grew up nearby in Sacred Heart, during the depression days. After college, she came back to teach high school English in Echo, a small town 23 miles east of us.

Phebe's life-long habit of keeping a journal makes it possible for her to recall and write about people and events of the past in great detail, to recall how she felt and thought. The magic of many of the poems comes from the way the Phebe of the present meets the Phebe of the past who wrote the journal entries. It's time travel, without the usual complications. Wouldn't we all like to pick a single day in our life and watch ourselves being that other person we were? And wouldn't it be fantastic to know what we were thinking as well? Phebe does it all the time in these poems. She illuminates the past and makes it part of her present. WHY STILL DANCE is a poetic memoir that covers 75 years of her life.

Phebe's father was a very strict Lutheran pastor, besides being a Midwestern male. Even when he is not named, he is often present in her poems. I like to imagine her father coming back from the grave long enough to see his wayward daughter behind a podium reading her poems to an enthusiastic audience. I see him, in character, thinking he might just nod at her before going away again, but I hold out the possibility that he would hug her tightly in front of all those people, knowing then what we in Minnesota have always known, that Phebe has a ministry of words and love and laughter.

Phebe's first book, SACRED HEARTS, was till now the only place fans could read her poems. But here it is, what we all have been waiting for, WHY STILL DANCE. It is no joke that Midwestern men (yes, I mean me) are reluctant to express their emotions. But I am willing to stick my neck out and say that the poems in WHY STILL DANCE are so good that when I finished reading them, I wanted to weep with joy at what Phebe Hanson had done with words and with her 75 years of life.

Howard Mohr

Contents

Dance

Why

Still

Dance

Dancing In The Dark

I watch my mother help my father
into his Prince Albert coat,
worn only for weddings or funerals,
the coat whose tails dip elegantly
below the backs of his knees.

His voice changes into that of a movie star,
his Norwegian accent floats away over
the cornfields. No more sinners called
to repentance. No more bodies committed
"ashes to ashes" and the hope of life everlasting.
No more cups of communion grape juice
offered to the chapped hands of Lutheran farm women.

You can do it, daddy!
Remember how you played cards with your
brother when you were a boy in Norway?
Remember when you smoked in the cemetery,
whistled at the girls as they walked by?

You can dance in your Prince Albert coat
into my movie, leap out of your practical Model A Ford,
drive straight out of town in a white convertible,
top down, your coat tails fluttering in the wind.
You can sit by the side of a kidney-shaped
swimming pool, your hand around a dark glass of whiskey.
After dinner you can dance with my mother, her white
satin gown clinging to her breasts and thighs.
You can dance out of the ballroom onto the patio,
watch lights glint in the Hollywood palm trees.

As I pass your room on my way to bed,
I see your Prince Albert coat, wrinkled and mud-caked
from the country road your Ford got stuck in
on your way home
from Mrs. Knudson's funeral.

Wild Nights

– for Emily Dickinson

Sitting on the shore of Lake Waupagassat, gazing out to the water, I am transported back to Green Lake Bible Camp near Spicer, Minnesota, summer of 1943, and I can feel myself in that dank dorm cabin filled with bunk beds and I can hear Miss Greta Swenson, our counselor and student at Lutheran Bible Institute, leading us in prayer, while Mavis Strindholm, my best friend that year, she of the short black naturally curly hair, she of the long slender neck and willowy figure, she and I poked each other during the prayer because Miss Swenson was using the very phrase we two cynics had made fun of many times: "Dear God, our Heavenly Father, may these precious young girls find the Lord Jesus Christ as their personal Savior..." and later we joked in our bunk beds about how we hadn't known Jesus was lost and then we launched into how cute Reverend Ivar Ingebretsen was and how we were surely going to respond to his altar call next evening right after Singspiration, even though we'd steadfastly refused on all the previous nights to come forward, but now we were going to say the Holy Spirit had moved us and we were going to walk right up to kneel at the altar, thereby announcing to the whole camp that we had found Jesus, because then Reverend Ingebretsen, who was only in his twenties and newly-graduated from Augsburg Seminary, would touch our hair as we knelt and pronounce us saved by the precious blood of Jesus as the pianist softly played and all the other campers, most of whom had already responded to the altar call on previous nights, quietly sang: "Just as I am without one plea, but that Thy blood was shed for me/ Oh Lamb of God, I come to Thee," and we drifted off to sleep dreaming of the touch of Reverend Ingebretsen's hand upon our hair, but our conversion didn't last long because when we got back to the cities, Mavis' old boy friend from Milaca, where the Strindholms used to live, showed up and Mavis reported to me after Luther League that he had kissed her and she had felt his "thing" jutting out and pressing right into her dotted swiss dress, and that very night Clarence Olson asked if he could drive me home from Luther League and amazingly, my dad said yes and as we sat in Clarence's car parked right in front of our house, he leaned across the steering wheel and kissed me, but since we were sitting down, I couldn't feel his "thing" but I did feel, as I told Mavis the very next day in school, his tongue pushing hot and hard against the roof of my mouth.

Somewhere I'll Find You

So we moved from my small town in western Minnesota
to St. Paul where I had to go to Murray High, a school
with more people than in the entire town of Sacred Heart,

and I had to walk two and a half miles every day because
there were no school buses, but it turned out to be not so
bad after all because I met a boy in confirmation class who

let me ride on the handlebars of his bike on the way home from
school and one Sunday my dad even let this boy pick me up
to go for a walk in Como Park, since after all the paths were

safe, filled with many families swarming with children, and
even though my dad knew the devil went about the city like a
roaring lion seeking whom he might devour, he let me go

with this boy because after all he was a Luther Leaguer and
we had sung together sitting side by side in church, "Yield not to
temptation, for yielding is sin / each vict'ry will help you,

some other to win / fight manfully onward, dark passions subdue /
look only to Jesus, He'll carry you through," but as soon as we
left my house this boy said he was going to take me some other

place I'd like very much and it was going to be a surprise so
off we went on the streetcar and new to the city I had no idea where
we were going until we got off and were standing in front of a

movie marquee and I said, "I can't go in. You know my father
doesn't let me go to movies. It's a sin," but he gently guided me
with his seductive hands, saying "Just come into the lobby to talk."

There below the sign "Somewhere I'll Find You," starring Clark Gable
and Lana Turner in a "torrid tale of love between two people caught
in the chaos of war," he persuaded me at least to go inside and sit

down and watch part of the movie and if I didn't like it, we could get
right back on the streetcar and go to Como Park, so I decided since
I already was in this lobby den of iniquity surrounded by posters of
Jezebel movie queens and devilish leading men, I was doomed anyway,
so I might as well go into the darkness with him and even let him put
his arm around me and hold my hand and that's the way it's been ever since.

Clouds

Lake Superior north shore cold but sunny
I sit on rocks drinking coffee in early morning
pure blue line of horizon steady before me

solitary gull flying toward clouds of suddenly dark
at sundown tornado warnings suppers hastily snatched
from table sliced tomatoes warm from our garden

quivering red upon flowered platter yellow
corn on the cob nearly sliding off as we grab
plump sun-suited baby from high chair

while rest of us children follow mother and father
down to the basement to eat supper on laundry table
basement where we hang clothes in winter

where farmer dumps dry corncobs each fall and field mice
fly up from the pale husks and heat rushes from furnace
belly basement where we sit in the tornado terror trying

to believe what our father tells us that we are in
God's hands and He will protect us if it is His will
or if we die in the eye of his great funnel he has more

wonder in store so we need not fear and we gnaw
timidly on our corn our missing baby teeth leaving tiny
gaps in the rows of kernels little husks caught in our teeth

When Dad Had Lumbago

He couldn't bend down
to tie his own shoelaces.
I had to do it for him,
me with my mother no longer
around to tie mine.
She'd gone off to the cemetery,
one-way trip, so I had to learn
how to tie shoelaces,
at least my own,
but somehow it seemed awkward
to do it for him.
He was larger than life,
even at, away from his pulpit.
It was as if God had admitted
to some human frailty,
admitted there were things
even He couldn't do,
simple things you'd ask
an eight-year-old
to help you with.

Valentine

Valentine's Day 1934 and my parents have invited the new minister,
his wife and two little boys to our house for supper and I'm excited
because we hardly ever have company and I'll have new playmates,
minister's kids like me who'll understand what it's like to be watched.

My mother has been cooking and baking all day, roast chicken, clover
leaf rolls, apple brown betty and we'll have buttered carrots and red
cherry jello salad mold with fruit cocktail embedded like jewels in the
shimmery mound and now I'm sitting in the breakfast nook watching

mother peel potatoes, watching the brown skin curl away from the
smooth white bodies, watching her cut them up to boil and later
watching while she presses the tender pieces through our potato ricer.
At supper we children are allowed to sit with the grown-ups but daddy

has warned us not to talk, so all I can do is sneak looks at the Qvistad
boys, Olaf my age and Søren the same age as my brother David and
after supper daddy tells me it's time to go the Johnson's for milk and
says maybe Olaf would like to go with me and maybe Mr. Johnson

will even let us watch him milk his cow, so we bundle up in our onepiece
snowsuits and stocking caps and tug on our overshoes and daddy
hands me the tin pail and we go off into the snowy, star-filled night.
It's only two blocks, but they go on forever because neither of us can

think of anything to say and I can't wait to get inside the Johnsons' warm
kitchen where Mrs. Johnson will surely hand us each a ginger cookie but
when Mr. Johnson spies Olaf he asks me, "And who is this then? Is he your
new boyfriend?" and I do something so impulsive that to this very day

I am still amazed by my boldness. I call out loudly, "Yes, he is," and lean
over to kiss Olaf full on his lips and Mr. Johnson laughs loudly and says
"Well, what would your father say about that then?" and I grab the tin
pail and run like a crazy person down the snowy streets, forgetting Olaf.

Next day I make the mistake of telling my best friend Gladys Nerstrand
what I had done and swear her to secrecy but it is too good a story for
her to keep and she tells her sister Norma, a third grader, and soon it's
all over the school, so when I'm pulling on my overshoes in the cloakroom

or eating tuna hot dish in the lunchroom or taking spelling dictation from
Miss Sundeen our first grade teacher, I hear the whispers, "Phebe kissed
Olaf. Phebe kissed Olaf. Phebe kissed Olaf." and daddy was right – every
one is watching me and soon he'll hear what a shameless daughter I am.

Safe

Today I saw the bumper sticker again,
the one I've seen so often before:
IN THE EVENT OF RAPTURE
THIS CAR WILL BE UNMANNED,
but since a woman was at the wheel, I felt safe,
and she was safe too because she was driving
a Volvo, certainly much safer than I felt
that morning so many years ago
when I woke up early and lay in bed
listening to the silence of the house,
convinced myself Jesus had come in the night,
swooping down out of the stars to gather up
my mother, father, brothers and sister,
to fly them away into heaven, while I,
the naughty one, was left lying alone
in an empty house, but soon my sister
came back into bed from the bathroom and soon
I heard my brothers arguing about whose turn
it was to do the paper route and soon dad
was hushing them with his usual admonition:
"Jesus doesn't like it when you fight,"
and soon I heard my mother in the kitchen,
probably stirring the oatmeal, and I knew
I was safe, at least for awhile, and I had been given
another chance to learn how to be good.

Breakfast Nook

Breakfast nook, whose wooden arms surrounded me,
as I ate oatmeal, rich with brown sugar and bananas,
warm milk fresh from neighbor's cow,
no pasteurization in those long-ago days.
What a wonder we never got tuberculosis
like Lorene Edman, the girl next door,
who had to go live in the TB sanatorium
on the outskirts of Granite Falls,
inside that grey huddle of buildings
we glanced at fearfully when we drove by
on our way to my dad's country churches,
Black Oak Lake and Camp Release Lutheran.

Today I sit again in that breakfast nook,
slowly letting the oatmeal slide down my throat,
having to finish it before I am allowed to pull on
my one-piece blue snowsuit with its aviator-like helmet,
"like the one Amelia Earhart wore," my mother says,
her eyes dreamy and far away,
tall and heavy with child in her cotton housedress,
covered with a bib apron, the kind all mothers
wore then, the U-shaped neck flung
gracefully over her head each morning, apron
on which she wiped her hands and all my tears away.

Today my mother is still alive, mother I remember most clearly
the day she lay dying and asked me to sit down at our piano,
play and sing one last time the hymn she had taught me
"Jesus, lover of my soul, let me to thy bosom fly,
While the nearer waters roll, while the tempest still is nigh..."

Today she is in our kitchen stirring a pot on the
wood range and I am safe in the arms of the breakfast nook.
I am her only child, darling and doted-upon,
my brother David still unborn, puffing out her apron
like the bread dough rising in the oven.
My mother and I are alone in the kitchen and she sings
an old hymn, "Jesus lover of my soul," and I look up
into her eyes and ask, "Mother, what's a bosom?"

Peonies

She went down into the black cemetery soil,
and my father planted peonies on her breasts,
tenderly turning the fresh clods of earth as

though he were preparing his annual garden.
In the attic bedroom we shared, our bodies
fallen together in the sagging middle of the

old iron bed, she cried out that night, head
bursting with migraine, her stomach retching,
and awakened me to say, "I'm sick. Help me."

I walked her down the stairs to the bathroom,
supported her head as she vomited over and over,
washed her face gently, gave her a cool cloth to

lay over her forehead, guided her up to bed, where
we both fell asleep. Next I knew, my stepmother
was leaning over me, whispering, "Your sister

is sick, we're taking her to the hospital. You must
wake up. You're in charge now of the other children."
I watched out our bedroom window as our ancient

Ford chugged down the driveway, my sister a shadow
in the back seat, leaning against Olga's plump body.
In the morning the blank enormity of what they

brought back to our bleak breakfast table, to our
homemade bread, toasted and waiting in its bright
butter on our flowered plates, the red eyes of the

jelly staring at our pale faces, our sister gone now
in the flower of her first blooming, peonies rising.

After Seeing "Night And Fog"

I am eight when my mother
dies and dad sends me
to live with her parents
and I am afraid because
they speak Swedish or broken
English, have strange habits.

I watch grandma wave her arms
above the flame of her gas stove
to singe off the hated hair, and she
holds my small arm with its
fine blonde hairs, urges
me to join her in hairless beauty.

Downstairs Sheldon Goldberg
waits to beat me at Chinese checkers,
waits for my smooth white arms
to float above the checker board.
Will he wonder at the smell
of burnt hair?

Lutheran girl, Jewish boy,
what do you know
of burning, of warehouses
where mounds of hair
wait, stockpiled, unburnt, wait
to be woven into good German garments.

Naming The Restaurant

– Sacred Heart, Minnesota, 1935

There was a contest to name the new cafe on main street, so
my girlfriend Patty and I decided to stop playing beauty parlor,
where we took turns slurping wave set, a sort of gelatinous glop,
onto each other's hair, then combing it into thick movie star waves
held in place by sturdy black bobby pins. Instead we got into the
restaurant-naming business one humid summer day, while
the rest of America was sunk in the Great Depression,
hardly any one daring to dream of opening a new business.

I was the designated recorder because I'd won a pencil in a
Sunday School Bible verse memorization contest. John 3:16
was inscribed on one side and on the other a thought-provoking
question: "God loves you – do you love Him?" I scribbled
names as fast as we thought of them. Grapevines entwined
around the pergola house gently rustled in the slight breeze
as we excitedly called out each new name: "How about
The Plate and the Spoon? No – I've got it – The Gravy Boat!"

We knew all about the gravy poured over mounds of mashed
potatoes and roast beef stacked atop a slice of Wonder Bread.
"The Beef Commercial," it was called, and local business men
sat at the counter, hunched over it, silent and serious.
We marveled at those men, the banker and the John Deere
dealer and the owner of PAULSON'S MERCANTILE.
They didn't go home and eat when the noon whistle blew
as we did – they stayed downtown and ate beef commercials.

Finally, one of us came up with the most brilliant of all names:
THE CHAT 'N' CHEW CAFE. We shouted out the name in glee.
It sounded so right. We were sure we'd win and began
at once to plan how we'd spend the prize money.
But Gladys Knutson, who had the simple but brilliant
idea to name it after the owner, got the five dollars instead.
Now everyone called it CORRINE'S CORNER CAFE, except
Patty and me, who insisted on calling it THE CHAT 'N' CHEW.

Cottonwoods

In the cottonwood grove
behind Dahl's farm
the eyes of rusting cars
stare at me before
I crawl into them,
pretend I am driving;
power flows from the wheels,
I believe I am in control,
forget my mother's heart
lies fading in a little bedroom
beyond the rows of corn.

They have sent me away
from her dying
to play in the grove,
to whisper into the ears of corn
towering above me
as I sit between the rows
reading her letters
which say she misses me,
even though it is quieter without me
and my brother fighting.
He has brought her a goldfish
from the little pond
beside the pergola house
and laid it on her stomach.

Years later I return to the grove,
where the cottonwood trees
have grown scrawny,
but the old cars are still there,
their eyes stare at me,
unseeing and dead.

Accept Loss Forever

–from an essay by Jack Kerouac

Soft folds of my flesh ripple out
before me as I lie in soapy bath water,
flesh gradually formed through
years of filling my body with food
to protect me from
the long-buried bones of my mother,
my belly in old age rounder
than when babies somersaulted within,
my breasts once blessed by hungry mouths
and by loving hands of my husband
now long gone,
my babies long gone too,
while I remain alone,
drowning in memories,
but instead pull myself up
and out of the tub,
walk into the new day
remember with sudden clarity
a verse I heard my husband speak
years ago as I stood by our sink
sunk in sadness
"This is the day
which the Lord has made.
Let us rejoice and be glad in it."

Fishing

My father, born in Norway, loved to fish,
but I've always maintained I hated to, have
always sworn I would never do it, because I
I remember as a kid how I was left on shore

to take care of my brothers and sister,
remember the infinite boredom
of those endless hours we sat on the sand,
straining our eyes to see the tiny boat far out

in the lake where dad had dropped his line. How
we hoped to see him pick up the oars and row
back to us. So I am amazed when I come upon
my 1945 diary, the year I turned seventeen,

how often I went fishing, even begged to go.
"Dad took me fishing today, just the two of us.
I caught six sunfish," I wrote, "but dad caught
nothing." Try as I will, I can't remember that day,

so I decide to imagine myself back in the old wooden
rowboat on Lake Owasso, sitting alone with dad.
What did we talk about? Did he try to convince me
I shouldn't enlist in the Army Nurse Corps, a strange

vocational choice for me, since I'd gotten my first C's
ever in both chemistry and physics, but I was a patriotic girl,
wanted to do my part in our fight for democracy.
Did he try to talk me into going to Augsburg College?

After all, he'd come straight from Norway to attend
Augsburg Seminary, and he had always assumed I'd also
go to our Lutheran Free Church school. I fish for an old
memory, but no luck. It gets away without being caught.

You Were Right, Emily

The bustle in a house
The morning after death
Is solemnest of industries
Enacted upon earth,—

The sweeping up the heart
And putting love away
We shall not want to use again
Until eternity.

About the bustle you were right, Emily, for on the three times Death
visited our house, the bustle began right away with parishioners from
my dad's three country churches bringing food: oval casseroles of
macaroni and hamburger, flushed with home-canned tomatoes;
rectangular glass pans, holding dense chocolate cakes, deepened
with red food coloring, heaped with cocoa and butter frosting;

circular glass pie plates with lard and butter crusts, crimped carefully,
lightly browned in wood stove ovens, tart custardy lemon, crowned with
puffy tan peaks of meringue. Bustle of casseroles to comfort us for losing
our baby brother, John Phillip, taken by the furniture store owner
and placed in such a tiny casket just after he had learned to laugh aloud.
Cakes to help us forget our mother Hildur Linnea "gone home to be with

Jesus," our father told us, her 31-year-old rheumatic heart stopped forever
from beating. Pies to lessen our grief over our 14-year-old sister JoAnne Helene,
who spent her last summer afternoon sunning with her friend Susanna,
but awakening at midnight, gasping for breath, dead by morning.

All three of them disappeared into their caskets, and I stood, five years old,
eight years old and nineteen years old, watching my father scatter dirt over
them, entoning the ancient words: "Dust thou art, to dust thou shalt return,
in sure and certain hope of the resurrection," and again you were right, Emily,
for his words marked the putting away of our love until eternity.

My Father Mows The Grass

Dad's mower throws sprays of grass
into the big canvas catcher
summer evenings
as we kids lie on our backs
safe on the soft green he's already mowed.
Now he pauses with surprising silliness
grabs great handfuls of cut grass
throws them at us as we sputter
cry out in mock dismay
but go on telling each other ghost stories
set in small town cemeteries like the one
across from our grade school
or horror tales of kids who had pumped too high
on the school swings
with their dangerous chain links
had gone over the bars into another dimension
never seen again
off into the outer reaches of the sky
way beyond the Big Dipper
into ether that swallowed them more completely
than that other ether Dr. Dordahl used
when he laid us on his operating table
to remove our adenoids and tonsils
and now we fall into silence and wonder
as a shower of stars shoots across the sky.

Grandma X

"The modern practice of signing letters with a string of X's indicating an
equivalent number of kisses came about by almost universal illiteracy in the
Middle Ages. People who could not sign their names, marked documents
with an X and kissed the mark to affirm their sincerity."

—NW Airlines World Traveler (11-93)

You kissed me far too often that year I lived with you, desperate kisses,
wet with love and grief for me and your daughter dead at 31, and
you took me everywhere, on the streetcar to visit Mrs. Carlson

born as you were in Smaland, oh beautiful southern Sweden, the word
set you both to crying into your white linen handkerchiefs,
and you took me to funerals, knotted your handkerchief into a doll,

the way my mother used to when I grew restless during daddy's sermons,
and I kept my eyes riveted on that soft featureless face, stared into its emptiness,
so I didn't need to look at the waxen faces of the doll-like corpses,

as stiff and awkward in their narrow satin beds as I was in the dress
you bought for me so I'd have something nice to wear, because you
didn't think my dad had provided me with proper clothes, you never had

considered him worthy of my mother, because he was Norwegian
and selfish, made her struggle for years with an old wood range, didn't
buy a new electric stove until after she died and he hired a housekeeper,

and the dress you bought me was way too old for me, navy blue
watch plaid, polished cotton with puffed sleeves and a little peplum,
and spectator pumps with cuban heels, fit for an old lady.

When you signed the charge account slip I flushed with shame,
because you couldn't write your own name, and I stood beside you
at the counter in the Glass Block, Duluth's finest department store,

watching you shakily struggle to write a large and misshapen X.
You had never heard about kissing it to affirm your sincerity.

First Friend

Make a list of all the friends you ever had beginning with Delores Morrison,
the newspaper editor's daughter in her flowered beach pajamas, California dream
brought to the dry back yards of Sacred Heart, Minnesota, Hollywood blossoming
on little girls making mudpies from pump water and caked dirt
which wouldn't grow gardens that year, the two of you squinting into the sun while
her mother took your picture, your squat firm body against her tall slender one
you in sunbleached bangs, she more languid and foreign, seeming not to
belong to that town, exotic and worldly even at eight, up in her bedroom
which she shared with no one, an only child, you never having known the terror
of privacy, envying her room's movie star splendor, you lying on her
white chenille bedspread, playing doctor, taking turns, lying there in your
cotton bloomers and thin-strapped summer undershirt, you feeling her cool hands
pulling down your bloomers, then separating the lips of your vagina,
looking seriously at them as only a doctor would, Dr. Dordahl who never
that you could remember had looked down there, all he had ever done was take out
your adenoids as you lay under the ether swirls, spinning into infinite
colored concentric circles, waking to the smell which would not leave you
even when the bitter taste in your mouth and the soreness in your throat had gone,
bending over to smell the roses in your back yard, hoping their smell would replace it,
and now she was looking into the flower at the center of your body, where not even
your doctor had ever looked, and she was pretending to be your doctor and you
accepted the solemn look on her face, you pretended not to feel the strange joy of her
fingers there because she was your first friend and you did what she wanted you to do
because she was older and when she thought it was a good idea for the two of you to
squat over the little grate in the floor of her bedroom and pee there, you did that too
because it was part of the excitement of playing doctor, and only the next day when her
mother took you both into the dining room and showed you the ugly yellow stain in the
ceiling wallpaper did you know you couldn't be friends anymore and soon she moved
away and you never saw her again.

Dirty Boys

Mother walks me to the town park to play on the swings.
I don't know yet about the dangers of swings, because
DeVonna Nyquist hasn't yet told me, as she will in first
grade, about the boy who pumped too high, swung over the
top of the bars. "Guess what? No one ever saw him again!"

Now I only know of wild wind that rushes past me, pushing
laughter out of my mouth until I have to ask mother to take
me to the outhouse, where I am afraid to go alone, so she
who does everything I ask, comes with me into that murky
light where I sit on the warm wooden seat, stare at strange

words scratched into the walls. "Mother, what does f-u-c-k
spell?" She quickly diverts me, tells me not to pay attention,
says it's just something dirty boys have written. Even then
I know it has something to do with what boys have hanging
between their legs, like the time at the Sunday School picnic

when I saw Arnold Olson holding his white thing between
his fingers and then he sprayed water against the bark of a big
cottonwood tree. Next summer after my brother is born, I
watch mother dip cotton into warmed olive oil, wipe with delicate
strokes around his penis until it is clean, so very clean.

My Father's Hero

Six months since I moved to this apartment, and I'm still unpacking.
Today I unearth an old photo album where I've rediscovered a snapshot
I'd forgotten: my father sitting in one of the Adirondack chairs he
was fond of making. Surrounding him are his four children, each of us

holding aloft a giant vegetable, tomato, rutabaga, carrot, turnip
and dad proudly displaying an enormous cabbage, all grown
in the garden he conscientiously weeded all summer, always
attired in his black suit, vest, white shirt, tie, and one of those

soft felt hats with a little depression on each side, as if a child
had playfully punched it in. After he retired, we kids tried
to give him short-sleeved sport shirts for Father's Day, but
he always refused to wear them. "Not dignified for a minister."

His hero was Luther Burbank, mostly self-taught California
horticulturist who developed or improved over 800 plant varieties.
Dad was sure he must be inspired by God. Perhaps, given his
first name, he might possibly even be Lutheran.

Last June I visited Burbank's garden in Santa Rosa and thought of
my father as I bent to smell Luther's roses, fragrant and delicate
like the climbing roses dad planted on the white trellis he built
leading into our garden, where the giant vegetables flourished,

grown from Burbank seeds. Our guide tells us Mr. Burbank
always wore a suit and hat when he worked in his garden, showed
us a portrait of him painted by one of his many admirers, next to
a photograph of him taken with the Yogananda who in his

"Autobiography of a Yoga" tells of visiting the man he called
"The Saint of Santa Rosa." How glad I am dad never knew about
the pagan yoga's visit nor about the pamphlet written by Burbank
which I found in the souvenir store: "Why I Am An Infidel."

Cinderella

After your mother turns to stone,
you sit beside your father
in the high Model A,
driving to church in the country.
You sit in the front row,
singing hymns in Norwegian
to please him.

At home in the kitchen
you make Eggs Goldenrod
for him and your other children,
laughing as you blow crumbled yolks
at each other.

You are as good and as beautiful
as your mother.
Secretly you smile to yourself:
he needs no other wife.

When summer comes, you lie
aching and peeling with Scarlet Fever.
A hired woman brings you meals in bed.
You can go nowhere with him for weeks.

He heads his car away
from your quarantined house,
finds another to replace you.
Later, the new mother smiles
down at you from the high front seat,
while you climb into the back
with the other children.

Born Mean

been mean from the day she was born
this child was born mean

grabs the despised new dress with long sash they force her to wear
hangs its neck on doorknob pulls until the waist rips free tears it to
shreds so her mother can't use it even for a scrub rag

been mean from the day she was born
this child was born mean

goes into bathroom sneaks bottle filled with lye to clean toilet
runs to garden drips lye slowly over tomatoes her father's so proud of
watches them die writhing into their vines

been mean from the day she was born
this child was born mean

opens icebox door knocks over buttermilk watches it blobble over
meat loaf and baby food tips highchair with baby brother in it
doesn't bother to wipe blood off his tiny rosebud mouth

been mean from the day she was born
this child was born mean

races out back door lets screen door slam as she bursts through
hedge to neighbors who think new baby is so sweet messes all
their National Geographics out of their chronological order

been mean from the day she was born
this child was born mean

Attic

Mother has disappeared and I am
calling for her, wandering from room
to room, until I climb the stairs to our attic,

find her there, kneeling on the slivery
wide-boarded floor and think she looks
like "Christ in the Garden of Gethsemane"

who hangs in our living room. Above her,
white drops ooze from insulation between
rough-hewn rafters and I remember what

daddy talked about at his Wednesday night
Lenten services, Jesus in the garden sweating
drops of blood and I see drops like white blood

sweating from the rafters that hot summer day
and mommy is crying and praying over a letter
from her only brother Harry. Once I remember

hearing my parents whisper to each other about
Harry but I didn't find out until much later,
he'd left his wife, the mother of my only cousin

in America, Sheldon, who was exactly my age,
but whom I only saw once before he and his
mother disappeared out of our lives forever.

What I remember most about Harry's wife was that
she wore jodhphurs, wide-hipped riding breeches that
made her look like a movie star, so I didn't understand

why he'd marry a second wife who looked matronly
in the pictures they sent from Yuma, Arizona, where
they moved after the divorce. Three years later, when

my mother died, Harry didn't come to the funeral,
sent a telegram I found pasted into an old photo album:
"Sorry to hear of Hildur's death My sympathy to all."

Square Dance

Dancing is a sin, my father told me.
That's all there is to it. No ifs, ands, or buts.
No exceptions. Not even for the Square Dance Unit
at Murray High, St. Paul, Minnesota, May 1943.
So he wrote a note to my gym teacher,
a far-too-long note, explaining
the reason I must be excused from participating:
dancing was against our religion.
I read the note as I walked down Larpenteur to Cleveland,
past the fields of the U of M farm campus,
where the little shoots of barley and oats and flax
were just beginning to push through the moist black soil.
The note didn't mention how embarrassed
I was at having to ask to be excluded
from square dancing. The note didn't implore Miss Miller
to try not to call attention to me in front of all the other girls.
I was miserable enough in gym where we had to wear bright
blue one-piece bloomer-like outfits that I would often leave in my
locker for months until they emitted unspeakable odors.
We had to stand naked with all the other girls under icy cold
or scalding hot water of the showers whose sprays burst forth
with military vigor and before we entered we had to step into
a tall pail filled with oily yellow disinfectant to prevent athlete's foot.
But horrible as gym was, to be excused was worst of all.
The square dance unit lasted four weeks so I couldn't possibly
pretend I was squatting on the sidelines, my butt pressed against
the ceramic tile wall in a futile attempt to make myself invisible,
because I had "The Curse." Even the most sympathetic
wouldn't believe my period lasted four whole weeks.
Then the Sunday after the unit was over, dad took us all
to Sytennde Mai Celebration in Minnehaha Park where
native-costumed Norwegian-Americans squared danced merrily
to sprightly fiddle music and for a few minutes after the concert
as we sat eating potato salad and summer sausage sandwiches
at the park picnic table, my dad was silent. But then he spoke:
"Well, I guess square dancing isn't so bad after all. Maybe
next year, Phebe, it would be all right for you to take a class."

Why

Why She Picks At Her Cuticles

Because she feels that if she tears off
that last bit of rough skin, everything
will be perfect, and she will understand
the meaning of everything at last:
the soft curve of orange cat
on the black canvas sling chair
shaped by the bodies of their children,
the philodendron and the Swedish ivy
on the sun room floor
which have stood side by side
so long their leaves now grow
from each other's stems,
the clear voices of three girls
passing by on the sidewalk,
voices low and conspiratorial,
yet the air so clear and bright
it carries every word to her ears –
"Do you think he really likes me?"
the sun-dappled grass, each blade
swaying in a different breath of wind,
the bird making that elm tree
come alive with an unexpected rustle
of bark-colored feathers,
and the man across from her,
behind his newspaper, about to speak
after a silence of many years.

Sex Education

Sex when I was growing up was not only
wicked but furtive, never talked about
except in whispers in bathrooms or
locker rooms, so when I had children
I determined to be different. Their sex
education would be straightforward,
no nonsense, but wholesome.

"Sex is natural and good," was one of
my famous statements, thrown back
at me by my children when they reached
their teenage years. I was open and
honest when I talked about how men and
women came together, maybe even a bit
clinical, never shying away from words
like penis and vagina and sexual intercourse.

Maybe I overdid it because when my
daughter was in second grade,
she brought home a carefully-printed
story she'd written, marked "Good Work"
by her enlightened teacher, a story
entitled "Mr. Penis and Ms. Vagina."

This was in the nineteen sixties when we were
riding toward The Sexual Revolution and
Minimalism, that odd cultural pair, and I
ordered these dolls from Creative Playthings,
rectangular and wooden with balls hanging
from little leather thongs and a tiny dowel
for a penis and two shiny nail heads for
the woman's breasts, a hole for her vagina
exactly the size of the dowel. My kids
actually played with these dolls, neighbor
children flocked to visit them, and the dolls
still bear the marks of many playtime hours.

When I found them again after they'd rested
for years in a basement storage room, my son
looked at them and shook his head. "Mom,
you're lucky we all turned out fairly normal."

To The Woman At The Retirement Center

You tell me when you were eight, newly arrived
from Czechoslovakia, your teacher made you memorize
a poem that began "I remember, I remember
the house where I was born." Stranger
to our language you proudly learned all the verses,
practiced them over and over in front of your mirror,
but at the program when you stood to recite
in front of all the parents and other students,
you got as far as "I remember, I remember,"
and forgot all the rest and had to sit down shamefaced.

Now you live in this ten-story retirement center
where you cried most of the first month, so lonesome
for your son, transferred to another city, who couldn't
take you with him because his new house wasn't
big enough. Sometimes, you tell me, you slip away
from the recreation director who wants to teach you
how to turn plastic bleach bottles into bird feeders,
sneak up to your room, turn on the Bohemian radio station,
dance barefoot all by yourself, as you used to

years ago in the house where you were born.

How Old Are You

Ruby, my 9th grade reading student,
leans toward me across the table,
asks me, "How old are you?"
groans when I tell her,
"Oh nooo. You must feel bad
being so old."
Then she leans even closer
to ask that question students often ask,
the one I have never learned not
to answer: "Do you mind
if I get personal?"
"Not at all," I say, forgetting
that I'm in for trouble now.
She rushes on to her next question:
"You can't have sex no more now, can you?"
I stand up and say to all the startled kids
in the room (the other tutors have to stop
tutoring while I carry on), "Did you hear
what Ruby just said? She says you
can't have sex when you're old.
Well, how many of you read Ann Landers
this morning?"

They all read Ann Landers,
even the ones labeled grade level 3.2,
though Ann is supposedly 6.7.

"Well, her column was about
how we stereotype the old,
figure they're not like the rest of us.
That's called ageism." My voice rises now.
"And it's just as bad as racism and sexism.
Ann says old people can have sex
as long as they want to, or
as she put it, 'As long as you use it,
you won't lose it.'"

Then they all laughed,
even Ruby, and it was the last time
she ever got personal with me.

Words

When you struggle in the door at night,
exhausted and faint from explaining
too many times to too many students,
and want only to lie on your couch and breathe,
your students crowd into your living room,
pour out of the kitchen, waiters with towels
over their arms, pert waitresses in frilly aprons,
bearing tray after tray of words,
words that have been on your counter and
in your refrigerator for weeks,
words dripping with juice,
words dry and tough to the tongue,
moldy words, over-ripe words,
sickeningly sweet words.

They keep bringing them in,
stack the trays on your coffee table,
then on the carpet when they run out of room.
You are expected to eat all these words
and tell them what grade they deserve.
You are expected to pass judgment on their
precious words, heaping plate after heaping plate,
and you can't even complain,
because you have ordered them.

Why do people always bring food
when there has been a death in the house?

Sturdy Arms

"You've got sturdy arms," my blind date said,
a student from Norway studying to be a missionary
to Madagascar. I was pretending to study English Lit,
but really on the alert at all times for a suitable husband.

"You'd make a good worker out on the mission field,"
my date went on. I stood on the steps of Sivertsen Hall,
Augsburg College, a few blocks from where the Mississippi
River flowed past to the University of Minnesota.

That's where I should have gone, I thought, where I'd meet
atheists and agnostics, studying to get rich some day, and when
I married one, he'd hire cleaning women so I could sit for hours
in my room, my sturdy arm writing poem after poem after poem.

A Cat Is Not A Person, You Say

– from the first line of a Gunnar Ekelof poem

And you ask yourself is it necessary to save him
after you find him in your basement laundry room,
lying on a pile of dirty clothes,
near death, silent and gaunt, both jaws swollen
with wounds from fighting for love in your back alley?
Shouldn't you let him die in peace?

But you wrap him like a baby in a soft flannel blanket,
carry him to the Animal Medical Center
where you cry with your daughter as you sit together
in the waiting room, holding his still body,
afraid he might die before the veterinarian calls you in.
You spend hundreds of dollars on him, for
anesthetics, surgery, overnight boarding at the clinic.

After you bring him home, you have to squirt medicine
down the little drains in his neck for three days,
poke pills into his unwilling throat, take him back to
the vet to have the sutures removed.

All this for a cat? you say. All this to keep that pile
of orange fur rising and falling on top of your radiator?
Is it really worth it? You hear your
own voice answer out loud: "Yes, oh yes."

34

Sacred Heart

In Sacred Heart, Minnesota,
we Lutherans
barely knew the Catholic kids.
Their mothers smoked Camels,
played bridge in the afternoons
instead of Ladies' Aid.
Their fathers, lying under their Chevvies,
said, *goddamn*, cursing the motors to life.

But we build bird baths of cement,
pressed splinters of broken bottles
into their wet breasts.
Hosiery salesmen driving through
to the Cities marveled.

We gave hoboes
who asked at our backdoors for food
glasses of buttermilk
because it was good for them.

When I was eight, a big Catholic kid asked me
up to his garage loft to see his crucifix.
Even then I knew that the Lutherans are justified
by faith alone,
and kept my legs crossed.

Skating Dream

It's been so long, you're not sure
you can still do it,
but the ice stretches before you,
not the rough ice
of your small town childhood rink,
but a smooth glassy plain
that goes on and on,
like Hans Brinker's Zuider Zee.

You strap on your father's skates,
even though you used to
make fun of them because they came
from Norway, were quaint and old-fashioned
but now you glide down the ice in them,
proud of yourself because
you haven't forgotten
how to skate after all.

You revel in wind and freedom,
until an errant twig catches
your blade and you fall straight through
the ice into the sea,
but miraculously you don't drown,
are seized instead by a sudden
lurching that turns the world over
and you rise up
to the surface, regain your balance,
go on skating as if
you'd been doing it all your life.

Santa Lucia

December 13, 1938,
my grandparents
give their yearly party
at the church in Duluth where
my grandfather is custodian.

Everyone has come to honor
Lucia, strange saint for Swedes,
virgin and martyr of Syracuse,
whose fiancé denounced her
when she became a Christian,
ordered boiling oil and burning pitch
poured over her stubborn head.

But on this night I am ten,
know nothing of that other Lucia,
know only I get to put on
the long white choir robe,
tied with red satin sash, get to wear
the crown of candles that remind
everyone of the light Lucia brought
when she appeared to Swedish peasants
bringing bread during a famine,
which is why Swedes celebrate her day,
bake saffron-spiced lussekatter
and appoint a young girl to play her part.

I am afraid as grandma places the crown
on my head and lights the candles,
afraid they will set my hair on fire,
but I walk in slowly, head held straight,
carrying the sweet bread shaped like cat's eyes
to remind us of the light Lucia brings again
to all the Swedes gathered in
Gloria Dei Lutheran Church
that long-ago December night
just before the world burst into flames.

What I Could Do, I Think

Today I want to shuck it all,
hit the road and never come back.
Oh, I know we've had a mild winter, but already
I've got a bad case of spring fever
and want to hit those gravel country roads
in a pickup, for which I've traded in my Toyota.
I'd leave everything behind except my journal,
make a quick getaway, maybe work as a waitress
in some small town cafe.
So what if I haven't been a waitress since I was 20.

All right, then, maybe I am too old to be a waitress,
but not so fast – I've still got my lifetime
high school teaching certificate so I could always teach,
and I believe I could learn to do
almost anything else, if I really had to,
like maybe brain research, for instance.
Once I watched a NOVA episode about the discovery
of a chemical substance in the brain
identical to or very much like morphine
and as I watched those lab technicians do their jobs,
I thought: "I could do that. I could grind up
rat brains, put them in a centrifuge,
go home and wait for the results." Then when people
asked me at parties,
"And what do you do?" I could say,
"Brain research, that's what I do. Yes, that's what I do!"

Nursing

Now I mostly remember
    how hard they pulled,

the unbelievable strength
    in those small mouths,

and the smell of sour milk
    drying on my dress,

the sunlight that fell
    across our bed

early mornings when I lifted
    them out of their cribs

to nestle them between us
    as they suckled, and

how I worried they would
    never get enough

because your mother told
    me to feed them formula

"so you can see exactly how
    much they're getting."

Nursing took up all my time,
    eating nutritious foods,

drinking gallons of water so
    the milk would flow freely.

I remember thinking surely God
    would protect me, not let me die

while I was nursing. It was the
    only time I felt really safe.

Wedding

We have no wedding pictures because you said we
didn't need a photographer to document our marriage,
flash and snap interrupting exchange of sacred vows,

because we'd keep the day's images forever in our
minds without benefit of camera, and furthermore
all the people in those wedding pictures look alike:

"We can always buy some used pictures on our 25th
anniversary, ones so faded from sun on the window display
no one can tell the bride is not you, the groom is not me."

And you were right. I still have those images forever
engraved in my mind, along with images from before the
ceremony when we stood together at Sears Roebuck

catalog counter ordering our plain gold rings, because
you had convinced me Thorstein Veblen was right about
conspicuous consumption and so instead of a diamond

engagement ring, you bought me a Singer so I could
make my own wedding dress, helped me pick out fabric
at Amluxen's and seed pearls to sew on my Juliet cap

from which my veil floated, and I can still see you at
the altar in your navy double-breasted suit with wide
lapels, also ordered from Sears, and I can still

see the reddish gold hair on your hand as you placed the
ring on my finger, the ring that now rests in the dark of
a little heart-shaped box deep in the back of my closet.

Meat

I dream I go out to dinner with a visiting poet, his hair curling black into his beard.
I am pleased he seems to like me, wants to have dinner with me.
We stand at a long counter ordering beef to go for my children, thick rare slabs.
The order comes to $4.58. I write the check. They dish up the meat in countless
black cast iron pans, rows and rows of them, more meat than we can carry between us,
so much meat, too much meat for the children.

We began to load the meat onto carts and then onto elevators, for now we
seem to be in the lobby of a dingy and mysterious hotel. The poet is on the elevator,
which has stopped a few feet below floor level and I am handing him down the endless
pans of meat. It takes forever. I know we will never get to dinner.
I think of Sisyphus. We are like Sisyphus! I am pleased to be dreaming an archetypal dream!

The poet is in the corner of the elevator and as I each down to hand him
yet another pan, I accidentally unhook a latch that causes the elevator to drop almost
an entire floor and the poet lurches, loses his balance. I can still see him, below me,
surrounded by the pans of meat. Furious, he is furious at me, shouts and shakes his fists.

Now I am in the bedroom of an old farmhouse in the midst of a snowstorm. The poet
has a new plan for getting the meat into the house. He has hooked the pans together,
an endless chain of cast iron pans, each with its steaming chunk of rare roast beef,
and he is climbing up the long sloping roof toward my bedroom window,
pulling the pans with one hand, dragging himself slowly up the roof with the other.
I lean out the window to offer my hands to help and he grasps them with both of his,
forgets and lets go of the pans. They slide off the roof with a frightful clatter.
He looks back, loses his balance. I can still see him, below me, surrounded by the pans of meat.
Furious, he is even more furious with me, shouts and shakes his fists.

I go down into the snowy farmyard below where many people are doing farm chores.
I am in a Breughel painting! I am pleased to be dreaming of Breughel! I look for my poet.
He is going through piles of manure and straw, looking for the meat. He will not look at me.
I feel great sadness, know the meat by now is ruined, that we will never go out
for dinner, that the children will never get their meat, so I leave the farmyard, go into the
house which is elegant and heavy with antique furniture, Russian in feeling. I am in
a Tolstoy novel! This is truly a high-class dream! I pass through the dining room into a small
dark room at the back of the house. It is a room in our old house in Sacred Heart,
and back in a corner a woman lies on our old daybed, napping. I walk over to her, kneel
beside her, tell her of my sadness. She awakens, sits up in bed, turns to me. It is my mother,
dead these many years, come back to comfort me in my dreams. She offers me
a pan of meat, tender and succulent, sizzling hot, from a table beside her bed.

Kierkegaard

You handed him over to me in the Greyhound Bus Depot
summer I left for Norway. He traveled with me on that
Stratocruiser filled with fellow SPANNERS—Student Project
for Amity among Nations—whose motto radiated sweet idealism:
"Better to light one candle than to curse the darkness."

On the plane pre-seminarians from Gustavus and Augsburg,
philosophy majors from St. Olaf, were all reading
him, too. It was nineteen hundred and fifty, the
middle of the twentieth century, when all of us
girls would do anything to get a man - yes, we were
girls and they were men. I thought I could
kill two birds with one book. If you did not come
through with a marriage proposal after my brilliant
and witty letters studded with references to SK,
as we in the know called him, one of my plane mates
might see me reading *Purity of Heart Is to Will One Thing*,
and decide I would make the perfect soul mate and possible
wife, or later when I got to Oslo, some Norwegian student
would notice me in a konditorei, drinking coffee and reading,
would glance at me from his table and immediately fall in love.

Later in our dormitory beds at the Studiehjemmet for
Unge Piker—the Study Home for Young Girls—we girls
talked back and forth: "How far did you go? Did you go
all the way?" I came close that summer, drinking my first
glass of wine in Ingar's room, smoking brown cigarettes
on a bench overlooking the harbor, feeling for the first time
a man's hand enter my blouse to touch my nipples.

But I never went all the way, because at the last minute I always
remembered you and Kierkegaard, so I spent the rest of my summer,
reading *Fear and Trembling*, dreaming I was your Regina.

Hat: My Old Babysitter Speaks To Me On The Como-Harriet Bus

Oh, how you look like your mother and you laugh like her too.
You know, I usually hated baby sitting but I always loved to sit
for your mother because she was such a free spirit. Did she ever
tell you about the time she was walking along on her way to the
grocery store and found some peanuts in her pocket? She thought
it would be fun to throw them up in the air and try to catch them in
her mouth, and then realized a man from your dad's congregation
was watching from across the street. Oh how she laughed at herself!

I loved to baby sit at your house, too, because your mother always left
such good things for me to eat. She made the best fudge, real creamy,
with walnuts the way I liked it, and she always left a big plate out for me:
"Help yourself," she'd say, "eat as much as you want."

Once my parents took your parents to Minneapolis for the day.
After they ate lunch at the Forum Cafeteria, they went to Dayton's,
where your mother tried on a hat she wanted to buy real bad.
It was real unusual, large-brimmed, with a long curving feather, and
your dad had a fit, I guess, told her she couldn't buy that hat,
it wasn't proper for a minister's wife. "It will call attention to yourself,"
he said, "and it's too worldly, looks like a hat a movie star would wear."

Your mother wanted that hat so bad that my dad spoke up, even
though he was a little afraid of your dad, him being a minister and all:
"Let her have it, Reverend Dale. It looks good on her. Let her buy it."

And you know, your dad had to give in. Maybe he was afraid of
offending one of his church members: "Oh all right, Hildur, if
you want it so bad, I guess you can go ahead and buy it." Later
your mother told me she spent her own money to buy that hat,
money that her parents had sent her, but I don't think she would
have gone against your dad, though. But do you know what?
She wore that hat everywhere, even to church, where she always
sat in the front pew, her being the minister's wife and all.

Grooves

All day I've been cleaning dirt out of grooves,
grooves on the grease-filled knobs of my gas stove,

barely-visible grooves on the handles of my sink unit,
three of them in each of the eight chrome handles,

grooves on my formica kitchen table to be dug out
patiently with a toothpick, daydreaming all the while,

finely-carved grooves on our dining room cupboards,
twenty four grooves on the chair rungs, rubbed with oil,

grooves on mopboards, across doors, along windows,
around the newel post of the ornately-carved staircase,

grooves in the bathroom between each of the seven hundred
and twenty tiles, grooves which must be carefully cleaned

with soft cloths dipped in sudsy ammonia water or sprayed with
Lysol and then wiped off with old rags cut from flannel nightgowns,

and finally grooves on the white radio in our bedroom, twenty-two
grooves to be cleaned with moistened Q-tips. How will I ever get

the dirt out of all these grooves in my household objects or out
of the grooves worn into our faces from trying to learn how to love?

Frog Prince

Frog Prince leaps from his
crossword puzzle, tries to catch
Princess off guard as she stands by the sink
peeling potatoes.
She ducks just in time as he crashes
into the window above the sink, gets a
nasty cut below his bulging right eye.

"Serves you right," Princess snaps.
"I can't do anything about your spell.
Face it. It's permanent. You might as well
learn to live with it."

That night in bed he tries to loop
one slimy leg slyly around her thigh.

"Nothing doing, F. P. I'm into this article
in Ms. and I'm going to finish it."

He turns his back to her, ·
croaks himself softly to sleep.
She awakes to find him sitting
on her stomach, eyes staring, pleading.

"Don't you dare touch me," Princess warns.
"I'm covered with warts from the last time,
and what good did it do you?
You still look like a frog to me despite
that ridiculous mustache
you've been trying to grow."

Coming out of the bathroom,
mustache partly gone, razor
clenched in his forelegs, blood
splashing from his throat, he falls at her
bare feet, leaps one desperate bound to her
breast, clings, catches frog feet on her nightgown.

She opens her mouth to kiss him at last,
tastes warm human blood.

Why I Love January

Everyone else hates it. Those who can,
leave for humid Florida or bone-dry Arizona,
take off right after Christmas.

Not me. I love Minnesota in January.
Love looking out window at tree's stark branches, love
tall chimneys poking up from jumble of houses other side
of my alley. Love how snow clings to roofs, softening their
drab asphalt shingles, love how snow mounds over
yellow daffodils and red tulips and blue anemones,
not dead but sleeping in Fran's garden, love the empty
whiteness marked only by animal footprints,

and the footprints of Faina, who brought from Russia
her love of hanging bedding
in crisp winter air. Look! Even now she is throwing
her down comforter over the line
strung from mountain ash to linden tree.

Love brilliant blue sky, love sun's unbearable intensity,
love most of all telephone poles, their wires carrying
messages to and from all whom I love.

Dayton's Sky Room, 1949

Longsleeved grey uniforms with white cuffs, heavily-starched white caps,
well, not caps exactly, more like tiaras that we bobby-pinned to our hair,

older waitresses scornful of us girls whose hearts weren't in our jobs,
only working to get through college, while waitressing was their career, one they

took great pride in, earning incredible tips because they were usually
the lucky ones assigned to the Oak Grill, dark elegant restaurant adjoining the

Sky Room, where a woman was admitted only if accompanied by a man,
where the tips were always generous because men tipped more than women..

Oak Grill waitresses were confident, unafraid of the steak cooks, rough men
with short tempers who made me tremble whenever I had to order steaks.

I always hoped for a party of women who would order chicken ala king
with creamed peas, served with iceberg lettuce wedge and 1000 Island dressing.

One night I was unaccountably assigned to the Oak Grill and given a party
of three couples, every one of whom ordered steaks, rare, medium rare, well.

Modeling myself after the senior waitresses, I fearlessly called out my orders,
arranged all six of them in overlapping fashion on a huge silver tray,

the way I'd watched Inez and Bernice do it, proudly strode into the dining room,
tray borne aloft on my shoulder, already dreaming of my huge tip.

But when I tried to download it, as we say now, all six plates, like slippery
oval dominoes, slid slowly off the tray and crashed onto the tile floor.

The rest is a blur, except I remember slinking out that night, how I was
almost comforted at the sight of the three Dayton brothers, who always stood

at the exit doors to bid their employees goodnight. Somehow I believed,
if they'd known, they would've said, "There, there, it's all right."

Close Call

All my life my father refused to talk about
his boyhood in Norway. "No," he'd say when
I cajoled him for details. "I'm an American now."

The only thing he'd ever talk about was how he'd
ended up in Minneapolis at Augsburg Seminary,
the story of his "close call," as he referred to it.

He was the only one of his three brothers and sister
who emigrated. "He broke our mother's heart," my aunt
told me when I visited her in Norway many years later.

She gave me the picture she'd taken the day he left, the
day after Christmas, 1920. He's impossibly young, already
wearing his life-long uniform – black suit, vest, white shirt, tie,

ready to go off to America, even if his mother's
heart is breaking, because he had to fulfill a promise
he made when he got the Spanish Flu, summer of 1918.

"Twenty two million people died," he was fond of telling me,
"twice as many as died in World War I, but I didn't die.
When I was choking and close to death, my mother

called the village doctor who performed a tracheotomy
right on our kitchen table and I promised then I'd serve
God forever if He wouldn't let me die. It was a close call."

Close call, I say, echoing my father, now dead these 20 years.
How close he came to being one of the 22 million, how he
almost didn't make it to America, almost didn't spend a

summer in Duluth, preaching at the Norwegian Seaman's
Mission, almost didn't meet my mother whose youth group
was serving coffee and cake after the service, almost didn't

marry her, almost didn't make love with her that warm June
evening of 1927, the night I was conceived, in the white frame
parsonage in Bagley, Minnesota. Close call. Close call.

Movie Star

On the radio we hear the news:
Jean Harlow is dead.
We sit in the darkened living room
of our neighbor's house,
the Olsons', their shades
pulled against heat and grief.

The Olson girls sit crying
on their davenport,
tears dropping
on their *Photoplays*.
They hold the key
to my life, their shades
always pulled,
their living room
like the womb
of the many movie houses
I yearn for
but am never allowed to enter.
And they wear lipstick,
forbidden scarlet cream,
as though they were movie stars.
I watch them stroke the tubes
of Tangee across their lips,
their mouths bleeding
into bloom in their mirrors.
I dream of movielands
blooming beyond the cornstalks
unfolding outside in the July heat.

Joy Olson stands beside me
in the fourth grade picture,
her hair blond and frizzy as Harlow's,
her mouth ready for stardom,
while her heavy-lidded eyes
already seem to know
that the boy standing
in the row above her
will leave a baby in her
by the end of the movie.

Wrestler

You retired early from the Lutheran ministry,
had plenty of time on your hands, only 62,
with stored-up energy from sitting
for so many years, reading the Bible and writing sermons,
so you began to add apartments to your house
on Edgcumbe Road, turning the basement
into a one-bedroom complete with functioning fireplace,
although you were rather testy when tenants actually used
the fireplace, something you never did with the one
in your living room, preferring to keep it smoke and ash free,
and you converted the attic
into a snug efficiency, providing rental income
in your declining years, although you were not declining,
still did substitute preaching, always tape-recording your sermons,
always inviting me into your study to listen to them, even though
I objected: "I'd rather just sit and talk to you, dad."

You also took to watching professional wrestling on TV.
How strange to see you absorbed in images of writhing male flesh,
you who had denied me in childhood the pleasures of movies,
calling them carnal and immoral.

So today I am shopping at Gary's Red Owl –
they try to make the impersonal chains sound humanly-owned here
in Montevideo, Minnesota – and as I wheel
my cart slowly down every aisle on a desultory quest
for groceries I don't really need, my heart is suddenly gladdened
by the sight of a red school folder. It's THE HULKSTER
n tight electric blue trunks, massive shoulders and torso oiled and bronzed,
a World Wrestling Federation champion, holding
an enormous trophy, strategically placed to not quite cover his crotch,
and I buy the folder for you, father, whose flesh must by now
be mostly gone inside your casket. You'd instructed us to pick
the cheapest one there was, but the mortician said, "This one
is too small for Reverend Dale. He was a husky man, you know.
His shoulders are too broad to fit," and I realized for the first time
you had a body of flesh and blood, a body built like a wrestler's.

Why I Wore Black On My Trip To Norway, 1986

Because my friends told me I should be inconspicuous
since I was leaving the week after
our bombing of Libya and terrorists might
target me if I wore flashy clothes and besides, black would show
I had no heart for the trip since three weeks before my flight,
my back gave out and I had to lie flat on my futon,
desolate, alone and unwanted, without a husband.
I'd left him after thirty years, for reasons I could
no longer remember. How had I managed to end up
an "old maid," when I'd vowed
I would never be like Miss Paulson,
who lived with us after our mother went "home to be with Jesus,"
as our father always told us.
I didn't think Jesus looked like much fun
to go home to, at least not in the picture called
"Christ in the Garden of Gethsemane" on the wall in our living room.
Jesus looked real unhappy in that picture, praying with both hands
clasped around a rock and his head stretched upward
so he could look at his heavenly father, beg him to take away his suffering,
but God didn't pay any more attention to Him than he did to me
when I begged Him not to take our mother away because then Miss Paulson
might have to be our mother, and she was old and had skinny arms,
so how could she hug us like our real mother
who was soft and young and smelled like Camay soap,
the soap of beautiful women?
Miss Paulson smelled like kerosene because when she had a day off
from taking care of us, she would go to visit old man Sundquist and we teased her
that he was her boyfriend, but she blushed and said he was too old for her and
besides, she told us, "I'm an old maid, you know," and I decided

I never wanted to be an old maid, didn't want to turn out like her,
because maybe I'd even have to wear a black coat with a narrow fur piece
around my neck, a fur piece with pointed noses of two little
dead animals with black button eyes that stared out at me when
I sat next to Miss Paulson in church the day of my mother's funeral.

So here I am, fifty years later, after getting married, raising three kids,
always trying to be as unlike Miss Paulson as possible,
an old maid anyhow, limping off to Norway
with a bad back and a suitcase full of black clothes.

Chameleon

My daughter brings home
her classroom chameleon,
even though she knows
I do not want it.
She wears it in her hair,
lets it hang on her neck,
while she bends over homework,
lets it lounge on her ear
while she practices the piano.
Its blue-lined eyes,
half-hooded by ancient lids,
follow me around the room.
I know it does not love me.
She looks up suddenly
from her plate at dinner,
chameleon nestling
under her chin,
warns me: "Sometimes, mother,
when you open your mouth,
to laugh or eat,
it jumps right in!"

Still

Still

Spotted a book called *Still Here* by Ram Dass whose book *Be Here Now* won our hearts in the 1960's and this recent book is about surviving a stroke and he assures us he's glad he's still here, and so am I, glad to be still alive, twelve years after Wegener's, that wretched incurable disease got me in its clutches and still so eager for news I subscribe to three daily newspapers, *Minneapolis Star Tribune* because my daughter works there, *St. Paul Pioneer Press* because I live in St. Paul, and *The New York Times* because old as I am, I still want to keep my finger on the pulse of the artistic life of the nation and I still believe you can only do that if you keep up with what's happening in New York City and I'm still frantically clipping articles so after three hours of morning reading, my hands are blackened by newsprint and I still have all these clippings from years back I don't know what to do with and I'm still reading mystery novels and I'm still reading Billy Collins' poetry, and I'm still reading serious novels, too, although I still haven't finished *Middlemarch* but I just finished *White Teeth* which is almost as long, and I'm still running into people who don't know me very well and at a loss for words, ask me if I'm still writing and later at home, still brooding over that encounter, I am reminded of the Inuit artist Pitseolak who began painting in her 60's and said she'd lived her whole life not knowing she could paint and now she loved it so much that she'd still be painting after she died if they'd give her paper and paints and brushes and I'm still not sure where all this is leading but I'll still keep on writing because I remember what Jack Kerouac said in his famous essay "30 Essentials for Modern Prose," that when you couldn't think of what to write, you should close your eyes and "see picture better" and that reminds me that yesterday when I was shopping at Kowalski's, at the tail end of that odious festival "Grand Old Days," the carry-out boys were laughing at a drunk guy across the street who was flagging down passersby, trying to get them to buy his flat tire and I thought of something else Jack Kerouac said in that essay, but instead of keeping it to myself, I said it out loud to the carryout boys, "Well, it just goes to show that Jack Kerouac was right when he said, "Never get drunk outside your own house," and then I felt compelled to add, "Jack Kerouac was a very famous Beatnik writer from the 1950's," and they stared at me with vacant eyes until one of them finally said, "Oh," and picked up my bag of groceries and I still don't know where this is all heading, in fact, I think I may be at the end of my rope, which is of course a reference to the hangman's noose, and so after all I've not managed to push thoughts of my friend and what he did on the first day of Spring, further and further into the recesses of my mind, but I'm still mad at him, still can't feel any real grief at his death, still not willing to acknowledge it was anything but a cruel and hostile act against those who loved him, to hang himself in the middle of the night in his garage where his wife would find him and have to cut him down.

Peace For You

– 14 January 1991 (at the beginning of the Gulf War)

Peace for my friend whose daughter had all her fillings removed
because they were broadcasting evil messages about her.
Peace for my friend's daughter.

Peace for the men at the Moslem prayer service at Coffman Union
last Friday who prostrated themselves on the floor, presenting
their buttocks to us women sitting in the back of the room.
Peace for the world's women.

Peace for the man next to me on the AirDyne at United Hospital
Exercare who said let's get in there and do it right and bomb the hell
out of Saddam and have it over with in two weeks. Peace for the
woman who takes his blood pressure every few minutes and tells him
she doesn't believe he really means that.

Peace for 92-year-old Signe Burkhardt who lives happily alone in her
subsidized apartment on her $450 a month Social Security check, and
who cheerfully tells the TV interviewer she gets along just fine.
Peace for Social Security and subsidized housing.

Peace for the lilac bushes behind my grandparents' old house at 510
East 8th Street in Duluth, lilacs I remember as a child, still blooming
last June when I drove past on my way to Lake Superior's North Shore.
Peace for the rocks along the North Shore.

Peace for my friends who sat quietly beside my bed during my long
and mysterious illness, the comfort of their breathing enough.
Peace for all our breathing.

Peace for my granddaughters, for Caitlin who told me on the phone
a few days ago: "Emma and I can't talk to you now because we're
reading books with our mother and eating popcorn with butter and
nutritional yeast." Peace for books and nutritional yeast.

Peace for my grandsons, for Alex who said to his mother as he held
his six-month-old brother: "I want to keep Jacob forever and ever.
I don't want him ever to die." Peace for our fear of dying.

Peace for my grown children and their mates so they may make their
way in the world, even after I'm dead and can no longer give them my advice,
which I only offer so they won't make the same mistakes I did.
Peace for all our mistakes.

Eating A Mango Over The Kitchen Sink

It's the only way to do it, even though Melody, my Weight Watchers
lecturer, has admonished us against the over-the-sink method of eating:
"Use your best china and silver, sit down, light candles, eat slowly."

But a mango is a different story, impossible to eat except leaning
over the sink, tropical juice dripping down my pale Minnesota
        winter wrists as I gaze
out at snow raging against my windows, like the storms of my childhood.

How I used to love them, when everything shut down – schools, stores,
post office, bank, and churches. "I suppose the pool hall's open," my father said,
knowing some in his congregation preferred that haven to church.

Our whole family clustered together, joyful over a free day,
        and even my stepmother
seemed happy, made cinnamon toast and cocoa with marshmallows
instead of the slimy oatmeal we all hated but had to eat,

and my father postponed his sermon-writing to join us after supper
in the living room while we listened to Lux Radio Theater,
        forgetting homework,
sermons, the dirty clothes in the basement, waiting on the cement floor.

For once we were all contented, sitting together on our old
davenport, even though not one of us had ever tasted a mango.

Love Poem To My La-Z-Boy

Your mom wanted it out of the condo right after the funeral,
so you called me, "Do you want my dad's La-Z-Boy?" and I said,
"Boy, do I ever! I've always wanted one. When can I pick it up?"

"The sooner, the better," you said. "Mom's always hated
that chair but she couldn't get rid of it while dad was still alive,
because it was his favorite, the one he sat in to watch television."

So I called my son, reminded him once again how much he owes me for
carrying him in my womb for nine whole months, through nausea and
backache and shortness of breath and heartburn and tight Pendleton

jackets which I had to wear in 1955 because I was teaching high school
English and as soon as you found out you were pregnant you had to
resign, and how I labored mightily for sixteen hours to bring him forth

and could he perhaps at the very least find it in his heart to go over to
my friend's mom's condo and carry my newly-acquired La-Z-Boy
up the steps to my second floor apartment? "Sure, mom," he said.

A few hours later he came up the sidewalk to my front door bearing
the La-Z-Boy, which turned out to be surprisingly light, on his head
and shoulders, and ever since I begin each morning with a candle lit

to the memory of your dad, settle into the La-Z-Boy with my cup
of coffee, my journal and my Pilot Razor Point pen, and begin
to write the same incantatory phrase I use every day: "Here I am..."

Christmas Letter

Here I am, living in my Riley Row apartment, all sole alone, as my grandmother used to say when someone's husband died and the children were grown up and moved away. "She's all sole alone now, all sole alone," accompanied by a shake of her head and the mournful Swedish phrase: Stakkars liten! But being alone, after all those Christmases with husband and children doesn't worry me as much as the bigger worry that many of my friends wouldn't know I'd moved out and into a new life and all the CHRISTMAS LETTERS would go to him at our old address, he who never in 30 years sent a Christmas card. Some people make fun of CHRISTMAS LETTERS, but I'd have trouble entering a new year with no news of DeWayne who married Lorna, a woman I taught school with back in 1952, and whose medical problems have been detailed in their CHRISTMAS LETTERS for years, including a grueling hemorrhoidectomy and esophagal reflux surgery. I look forward as well to the letters from Dorothy and Marvin, who last year wrote of the whole family's trip to Hawaii for their airline attendant daughter's wedding to the airline pilot boyfriend and who arrived only to find the couple had quarreled so the wedding was off, but they decided to have a vacation anyhow and there they are drinking mai-tais together. Or would life have meaning if I didn't get CHRISTMAS LETTERS from Borghild, my friend who met a Norwegian during a summer study trip and he followed her to America and they were soon married, but he grew so homesick he went back to Norway for a month, and fell in love with a Norwegian girl and asked Borghild for a divorce. And surely I couldn't stand not getting another CHRISTMAS LETTER from my high school friend DeLores who has kids, all doing fabulously—a graduate student at London School of Economics, one with fabulous grades in medical school, another in Hollywood about to hit it big, and the 32-year-old still at home "trying to find himself," a fabulous person nonetheless. I don't have the heart to lose touch with all those old friends, whose lives once intersected with mine. I love to think of them at Christmas, out there living their difficult lives, yet never giving into despair, always finding in the midst of all their trials and sorrows, the time and the courage to write yet another CHRISTMAS LETTER.

Broccoli

Before my granddaughter Caitlin
started school, I'd ask her what her favorite
foods were and she'd always call out:
"Broccoli and tofu!" but now she's
entered the world of public education
and her tastes have changed. Last time
she slept over, she made sure I knew:
"Grandma Phebe, I still like tofu
and broccoli, sort of, but what I really love
best of all is white bread and M and M's!"

But I'm still eating broccoli, more than ever
since Bush banned it from the White House
and his presidential jet. In fact, the whole
country's eating more broccoli – consumption
went up ten percent after his boycott and even
Barbara allowed as how she'd always loved
broccoli and was willing to cook up at least
some of the gifts broccoli growers kept
sending to change Bush's mind.

How could Bush have guessed there'd be
a broccoli backlash, a great wave of support
for that underdog vegetable, that all across
the land, housewives and househusbands
would begin the great broccoli cook-in,
covering kitchen counters with mounds of
small dark green trees, turning them into
Buckwheat Broccoli Gudunov, Broccoli Quiche,
Broccoli Salad, Broccoli Chickpea Stew,
Broccoli Confetti Spaghetti, Broccoli Tofu
Stir Fry, Broccoli Strudel, Broccoli Garlic Dip,
and even Broccoli Upside Down Cake. Such
a backlash that perhaps all America will turn into
The Enchanted Broccoli Forest, through which
Bush will wander, hungry and lost,
slack-jawed and hollow-cheeked, unable
to find his way home.

Daren's Garden

I walk in the sunny prairie garden
growing between a farmer's field and
the Yellow Medicine River, worked in for years
by a grade school teacher who lovingly
grows seedlings in his small house,
transplanting them in spring to the beloved garden,
where old students abandon their cars
and couches and easy chairs and beer cans
and Daren plants flowers in and around
them as they slowly through the years
sink back into the earth.

High grasses wave in the wind and springy
mounds of dead leaves make paths for my
sandaled feet, grasshoppers thrum against
my bare legs and I stumble into gopher holes
that descend deep into underground passages,
connecting all our graves, and I think as always
of my long-dead mother who waits everywhere for me,
mother who read me the story of Persephone,
child who strayed from picking meadow flowers,
was kidnapped by the Lord of the Underworld.

In childhood dreams my mother's white hand reached
from her grave, calling me to join her, to leave
the hot sun and rushing prairie wind, and descend
with her into the dark tunnels and once again
I am tempted by the desire to let go of it all,
to leave behind the heartache and betrayal of this world.

I lean over to smell a wild rose, feel the sharp sting,
violent and deep, the stab in my neck, remember
my friend working in her garden, the bee sting
closing her throat, the 911 call, the medic's adrenaline shot
saving her just in time and now my own adrenaline
propels me into my car, across the grass-humped road,
to the main highway and I am heading back
to the city, singing loudly an old hymn

"Leaning, leaning, leaning on the everlasting arms,
Leaning, leaning, safe and secure from all alarms."
Soon I am humming down old familiar Highway 212,
getting out alive one more time.

Stones

My cleaning woman says, "May I ask you a personal question?"
but before I can answer, she goes right ahead and asks it anyhow:
"Why do you keep all these stones in baskets all over your house?"
She means my beloved rocks gathered on Lake Superior's shore.
"What good are they? Do you have plans to use them for anything?
Not that it's any of my business, you know, but I was just wondering."

I never wanted to have a cleaning woman but my friends insisted
when I got Wegener's Granulomatosis, a disease that burns holes
in the arteries, a disease that almost killed me in the six months it took
my doctor to figure out why I went blind in one eye, lost my hearing,
why my ankles and knees were swollen and painful, why I
had no appetite, why I woke up every morning certain I was dying.

After I left the doctor's office with my diagnosis, I sat in the Edina
Library with the Merck Manual and read about Wegener's, how it had
always been fatal, destroying lungs and kidneys, until the miracle drug,
Prednisone, came along, stopped the disease dead in its tracks.
In my purse was the prescription which would save me from certain
death. I left the Merck Manual on the table and headed for my car.

But now I still have this cleaning woman who's questioning my rocks
and she's waiting for my answer and I can't think of anything to say,
so I pick up a stone, smooth grey oval, encircled with pink veins of
quartz and stroke it over my face. "These rocks have no use except
to remind me of the North Shore, of its blue waves and sunrise skies.

Here, have one. You may keep it, start your own collection."

Below Zero

Awaken at 5 am to radio announcement: 13 below
with gusty winds bringing wind chill to 23 below.
Sudden image of my little grandsons waiting for their buses,
and they're not wearing caps nor mittens
because they're guys and they don't need to
dress warmly as their grandmother
wishes they would. Wait until 5:20 when my daughter
is sure to be up since she teaches an aerobics class
before she goes to work, but when
she answers the phone, I hear panic:
"What's the matter, mom?" and I realize
she thinks I have bad news, so I quickly reassure her,
"Oh nothing. I just heard on the radio it's bitter cold today,
23 below wind chill and I thought maybe I'd come over and
take the boys to their bus stop, maybe even to McDonald's first
for breakfast. Did I wake you up? I'm so sorry.
Go back to sleep honey and call me later," which she does
to tell me Alex and Jacob are excited that I'm coming over,
and they'll be watching for me so I won't have to get out of the car,
but when I get to their house, they don't come out, so I go in
and sit around in my down jacket until they're ready.

Finally off we go to McDonald's where everybody
orders sausage egg biscuits with hash browns and orange juice,
except me because my delicate elderly digestive system
has rebelled against fast food, a great sadness to me
who loves Egg McMuffins and the prices are so affordable
even a pensioner grandmother can spoil her grandsons,
and off we go a-munching to the bus stop corner
where as we sit waiting in my warm car for the bus,
Jacob remembers he's supposed to bring treats for his music class,
so I give him $5 and he dashes to the nearby store and
while he's gone their buses come and go
so I have to drive them both to school.

Next morning, it's 29 above zero with no wind chill,
and Alex calls to say they've overslept and missed their bus
and can I take them to school? So I throw on clothes, race
to their house, hustle them into my car.
They call out plaintively from the back seat, "We didn't have
time for any breakfast. Can we stop at McDonald's?"

Despair

"...and a certain persistence in despair finally gives birth to joy."
— September 15, 1937
Albert Camus Notebooks

Filled with the old despair, I sit alone this morning with a basket of
objects I've saved through the years. Idly, I stroke a shell, finding
comfort in the whorls spiraling toward its smooth pink heart.

As a child I lay on the Lake Superior sand of Park Point,
staring at the sky through half-closed eyes, squinting to visualize
infinity, word I'd learned from my endless hours of reading.

Was infinity like everlasting life or forever and ever amen,
something that goes on and on and on, like the girl on the Morton
salt box, holding her box, holding her box, holding her box?

Or like my life now, endless round of losing glasses, mislaying keys
to important doors, forgetting appointments with people I love, yet
never tiring of the perpetual spiral repetition, loving every new day,

beginning with that patch of sky and spires of cathedral and gingkos
that rise beyond my window, reminding me of words
on the spine of a book glimpsed years ago in Marly's bookstore:

"I Can't Go On/ I'll Go On."

Granddaughter, After The Divorce

Every Tuesday I pick her up
from her parents' green-shingled house
on the west bank of the Mississippi near Riverside Park
where we used to go on picnics
when we were students at Augsburg.

She's fifteen months old now,
born on her parents' futon
with a midwife in attendance
and I saw her mere hours after her birth,
looked down at that unbelievably tiny body,
remembered how I'd given birth to her dad
a few blocks away at St. Mary's Hospital
on March 25, 1956,
light snow falling, sadness in the afternoon
when we had to say goodbye so you could go to work,
and I was alone, the baby down the hall
in the nursery, getting to hold him
only when the schedule allowed him to be nursed.

Today when I carry our granddaughter
into the cold air, she holds out
her blue-mittened hands, announces "Snow! Snow!"
and I see snow for the first time all over again.
In my apartment she reaches into my basket
of Lake Superior rocks, solemnly picks up rock after rock,
hands each one to me in a ritual that continues
until all twenty-seven rocks have been passed back
and forth between us many times.

I miss her after she goes back to her parents,
during the week when I'm alone in my apartment,
and I miss you sometimes, too, because you aren't
around to share delight in her, the way we used to sit
on the floor together and play with her father, our firstborn.
Last night I dreamed about my granddaughter,
that she'd learned to talk in complete sentences
in only one week's time. "Grandma," she said
in a high clear voice that still rings within me,
"Nothing is ever the same. But sometimes it's better."

Crone

Carefully supported by my sturdy walking stick,
carved by an old Norwegian in Lutsen, I pick my way
down the incline to where waves crash against rocks,

settle myself against a sun-warmed stone that just fits
my body, gives respite for my stiff back. I spread
and lift my billowy skirt to let sun rest tenderly

on winter-paled legs, bend to examine
closely skin on knees and calves,
scored with fine wrinkles I can hardly believe are there,

preferring to believe my legs are unchanged since
childhood, legs hanging happily from monkey bars or
bicycling down country roads as I look for pussy willows.

Lame Deer says our bodies get so wrinkled as we age,
that we begin to look like the rocks themselves and the markings
on my legs do look, I think, like the ones on these ancient glacial rocks,

a thought I find strangely comforting. "Soon I'll be a crone,"
I say to myself, "an elder filled with wrinkles and wisdom,
and when even my walking stick can no longer

support my old body, I'll slide down the path, a gleeful
child again, crawl on the rocks like a baby new to the world,

toward crashing waves and endless sky."

The New Riverside Cafe (1970-1997)

Here I am at the New Riverside Cafe
on a summer Sunday morning.
I have skipped church to sit here
and eat heavy whole grain pancakes
stuffed with pecans and bananas,
soaked in genuine maple syrup,
probably tapped from maple trees
on a cooperative tree farm.

Worker owned and worker managed,
decisions arrived at only by consensus,
according to my son who will work here
for ten years after graduating from the U of M
with two degrees, one in speech
communications and one in studio arts,
and now I am here growing more torpid
with each bite of syrup, gazing at the

customers not one of whom is wearing
a suit or dress or high heeled or wingtip shoes,
not one of whom is aiming to break through
the glass or any other kind of ceiling.
In my syrup haze my heart is filled with love
for my son and all the young who dream of
a new world of peace and social justice,
who have left the majority culture behind.

When my last morsel has disappeared,
I gather up my journal and my book of poems,
saunter out to cross Riverside, wait at the red
light next to a young mother in tie-dyed
tee-shirt and flowing India print gauzy skirt,
with her flaxen-haired toddler dressed to match
her mother, and once again thoughts of a brave
new world suffuse warmth through my body,

until the toddler drops the box of Crayolas
she is carrying and all the colors – magenta,
sea green, goldenrod, robin's egg blue –
scatter onto the street just as the light

changes to green and then as I bend to help,
I hear the mother speak the words
which shatter all my hopes for the future:
"Get your shit together, Rainbow!"

Epiphany

My daughter and her sons stay overnight
because their father is ice fishing,
sitting in a dark house, line dropped into
deep water, waiting for tug that signals a bite.

We're watching a video when Leah remembers
she forgot to bring her Sunday School materials.
What should she do with all those four-year-olds
whose attention span lasts just a few minutes?

I suggest she talk about the three kings who came
so far to see Baby Jesus and to remind the kids
Baby Jesus' family was homeless like so many now.
Ask them if they know anyone who would visit

a homeless family today. Jacob, who's five,
a graduate of his mother's class, speaks up:
"I know about the homeless. Grandpa John cooks
chili and we serve it to them at his church."

So we decide Jacob can be visiting speaker in
the four-year-old class and talk to them about
the homeless and ask them to draw pictures of
the gifts they'd bring to Baby Jesus today if he

were born under the Mississippi River bridge
where no one would find him, except maybe
my ex-husband and my grandson, come to bring
them temporary cheer in a steaming pot of chili.

Fast Food

America, I love your fast food,
your White Castles with the little holes
in each of the square hamburgers,

allowing the meat to breathe,
your Big Macs everywhere the same
each one containing exactly

the same number of ounces of beef,
with the same percentage of fat,
each one quality controlled so that

were I to eat in Moscow or Beijing
I could count on getting 36 points,
in Weight Watchers parlance, of food,

five points more than my day's quota,
but what the heck, guess I'll have
a small fries, too, and perhaps the

shaker salad to salve my conscience.
But best of all I love your Subways,
and the story on Oprah yesterday

about the man who lost three hundred pounds
by eating two Subways a day, one at noon
with turkey, no mayo, and one at night,

all vegetable, no mayo, and there he was
with the only person who'd stood by him
during his fat days, his college roommate,

a slight young Asian American, who declared
earnestly he had always been able to see
beneath the fat to what his friend's true

character was, encouraged him in his weight
loss only because he was worried about
what all that fat was doing to his great heart.

For Now

— On My Houseboat, 4 July 1991

Try to forget the newspaper story about the
woman whose husband threw an iron at her
because she didn't press his shirts properly

and the 18-month-old baby girl taken
from her crib in the middle of the night
and sexually penetrated by a passing stranger.

Try to forget our troops in Saudi Arabia poisoned
by unknown gases and the homeless lounging on the grass
of Navy Island as if they were simply having a picnic.

For now lie on your stomach on the
cushioned bench in the rear of your boat
this blue Fourth of July morning

let the Mississippi undulate
at the level of your eyes, notice
St. Paul's tall downtown buildings reflected

like zebras in the river, watch slow
stately barges bearing coal push up
small cascades of white water

so your boat rocks gently
the tie-up rope creaking like the swing
on your hometown front porch.

Even the ambulance's screams sound languid
as you gaze at the American flag waving
innocently from your boat's deck.

Just for now forget everything but the
brightness of that flag's promise, the purity
of its stripes, the brilliance of its stars.

I Listen To The Radio In Montevideo, Minnesota And Think Of My Son Who Will Soon Be Thirty

Someone, it's Lois, I think, is interviewing the
new city manager, who's been here since October.
He's young, not even thirty, I guess, since he
informs us he graduated from college seven years ago
and he has a career plan which he tells about in
a quiet, totally confident monotone, how after being
a city manager in a small Ohio town, he decided it would be
good for his career plan to apply for the Montevideo job
because he felt a new location would be a challenge and
was delighted when he became one of the finalists and
even more pleased at the news he'd been selected for this
new opportunity which fit in so nicely with his career plan,
and he says he's now exactly at the stage in his career plan
where he wants to be, and I think of my own son, who will be
thirty next month and who has never discussed with me
his career plan beyond his desire to continue as an anarchist
working in a collectively-owned vegetarian restaurant on the
west bank of the university campus, tie-dyeing tee shirts
in gaudy and joyful colors in his back yard on summer
afternoons and raising with his serene and intelligent wife
my one and only, so far, perfect granddaughter, and as I lie
here recovering from a brutal and relentless flu, as radio
voices float over and around my dozing body, a memory
rises of my son the spring he was three, how he danced
the Horah at Temple Israel Nursery School, where he went
for two years until he almost forgot he was Lutheran,
persuading me at Purim to make Hamantaschen pastries
for all his nursery school buddies, how as he danced in his
short gray wool pants held up by suspenders over the white
cotton shirt I'd sewn for him from a Simplicity pattern, the
suspenders broke and his pants started to fall down
around his fat bare legs, but he didn't seem to care, just kept
leaping up and down to the wild ecstatic music, while he held
his pants up with his hands and never once stopped dancing.

Why I Have Simplified My Life

Due to improper handling,
that's what Terry,
my personal banker,
said when she wrote to tell me
she was closing down
my checking account,
but it's all right, Terry,
I've learned to work with cash,
come to prefer it actually,
those one hundred dollar bills
I always ask for
when I cash my pay check.
No one can ever change them,
and they simplify things
when one of the kids
asks for a couple of dollars.
I've given up my car, too,
or rather it's given up me,
and I always take the bus
or walk or drive my new
unfashionable three-speed bike.
My daughter doesn't want to be seen
with me, says I ride too low in the seat,
look like I'm on
one of those adult tricycles.
I've given up cigarettes, too,
way back on September 4, 1979,
at 11 a.m. I decided never to smoke again,
because I heard that my doctor,
my age and fat and healthy like me,
even though a terrific smoker,
had dropped dead of a stoke
while making her hospital rounds.
The things I've given up to simplify my life:
plans to read all the novels of Henry James,
to finish *Moby Dick* and *Middlemarch*;
I've given up ironing, meal preparation,
and most housework:
I've allowed my subscription to the *Village Voice*
and the *New Yorker* to expire,

along with the satisfaction
of having my finger on the pulse
of the New York art and literary scene.
I've had to give up my father,
who went to join my mother, sister, and brother
in that cemetery outside Sacred Heart, Minnesota,
one snowy November day.
Now that I've lost my last buffer against death,
there probably isn't anything
I can't learn to get along without.

Almost

In 1986 when I visited
        my cousin Esther in Norway
            she mentioned:

"One of our good friends
        is a poet. Perhaps
            you'd like to meet him,

although he's very old
        and very sad because
            his wife just died."

I hesitated, wondering
        if this was such
            a good idea,

an American poet
        who spoke Norwegian
            like a backward child,

meeting a local poet
        who probably wrote
            bad rhymed verse.

"Oh, I'd rather not,"
        I answered. "I guess I'd rather
            spend the day with you.

What's his name?"
        I added, trying to feign
            enthusiasm, however slight.

"Rolf Jacobsen," she answered,
        "but you've probably never
            heard of him."

Snow

First snowfall today
and I think of my son Rolf
who used to love the snow,
who loved to ski and winter camp,
but who lives now in Sarasota where
snow never falls and I remember
the voice of Kate my Florida
grandchild reciting a Robert Frost
poem to me on the phone,
the one about the crow shaking down
snow from a hemlock tree,
the poem that ends
"...and saved some part
of a day I had rued..."
and then Lis coming on the phone
"too shy to talk," her mother Ann says,
"but she'd like to sing you a song,"
and then the sound of her two-year-old
voice sweetly piping
"Angels we have heard on high
Softly singing o'er the plain"
and I stare out my window this grey morning,
imagine them with their ocean and
sandy beaches and palm trees,
and me with my snow-covered mountain ash
all joining in to sing the final
"Glo-ooooo-ooooo-ooooo-r-i-a!
In Excelsis D-e-o!"

Brand Names

"When to the sessions of sweet silent thought
I summon up remembrance of things past..."
— Shakespeare's Sonnet XXX

I am driving down Grand Avenue, hoping
for a red light, so I can put on my lipstick,
Revlon's "Mauve Mystique," whose smell
summons up my first date with you.

March 1, 1948. I wore Revlon's "Fire and Ice,"
borrowed from my sophisticated friend Irene,
because my father disapproved of any makeup
("Be happy with the natural color God gave you").

I wore a borrowed dress, too, a "Jonathon Logan,"
black crepe sheathe, long and sinuous and clingy,
and borrowed perfume, "Tigress" by Fabergé,
rich musky scent promising delights of the flesh.

Only my bra belonged to me, pale blue nylon
"Permalift," bought at Dayton's with money I'd
earned as a summer girl in White Bear Lake, and
matching blue panties, trimmed with delicate lace.

As I sat beside you in the Edythe Bush Theater
watching *Street Scene*, Elmer Rice's 1930's play,
the "Tigress" wafted up to us its message of passion,
while the "Permalift" kept my breasts firm and safe.

"Put brand names into poems," Jim White once
said to his class, and his poems are still alive even
though he's been dead now for twenty years, his
body crumbled almost to dust, as has my love for you.

What's left is the remembrance of all our years together
and the poems I write to keep the memories alive.

To The Gloria Dei Women Of The 90's

"Age puzzles me... my 70's were interesting and fairly serene,
but my 80's are passionate... I grow more intense as I age..."
— Florida Scott Maxwell

I get up before dawn, drive in winter darkness to my first meeting
with these women, mostly in their 70's and 80's, many living alone,
some widowed, some never married. Here they all are at church

early morning to drink coffee and eat Swedish cardamom bread and
watch a video on the famine in North Korea, then listen to a report
from Mavis who attended a legislative hearing about the shutting off

of food stamps to legal immigrants. She pounds her fist on the table:
"Our government is immoral. We claim we don't have money to feed
these people, but our pockets are full of money and our pantries of food."

Myrtle and Helga report on their trip to Guatemala. They studied Spanish
before they went so they could talk to the people in San Lucas and listen
to their stories. They speak vividly of Father Greg's mission, which our

church helps support, say his goal is to help the people buy land so they
can set up a coffee cooperative of their own and will at last be able to build
better houses & schools, have better lives for themselves and their children.

Linnea implores us to sign up for the Food Shelf Committee and Arlene
reminds us that workers are needed at the Dorothy Day Center and
Verna makes a plea for us to give money to her cause, "Adopt-a-Family."

I look out the windows as the dark sky slowly fills with light and hear
Doris make a motion that we need to change our name now to keep up
with the times and all agree to become Gloria Dei Women of the 2000's.

Old Folks Home

They never call them that anymore,
nursing homes mostly
or sometimes care centers,
but whatever they call them
I don't have the fear
so many of my old friends express
of being "put away in" or
"sent to" the nursing home.
Sometimes I think:
how restful –
no more expectations,
no more ambitions,
no more goals or plans,
no more worrying about money,
just giving over to the soft foods,
oatmeal with brown sugar,
tuna hot dish with canned peas,
creamed corn side dishes,
buttered cloverleaf rolls,
tapioca pudding,
grandbabies and greatgrandbabies
brought to see me,
not so I can carry them around to soothe their colic
but simply to hold,
to press my face against their soft cheeks,
then give back to their mothers.
Or older grandchildren pushing my wheelchair
into the garden along the lake,
later, the Luther Leaguers coming to sing
"What a Friend We Have in Jesus"
and a handsome young man playing the guitar
and leading our quavery voices in singing "Heavenly Sunshine."

But I'd also want books on tape, CD's of my favorite
music I never have time now to listen to –
Bach and Haydn, Brahms and Mozart,
videos I've always wanted to see,
art supplies so I can paint and draw and make collages.
All my journals, of course, so I can relive the years
and keep writing new stories and poems.

I'll need my iMac too, that trusty purple friend.
Maybe I'll offer to teach a journal-writing class.

Maybe I won't go to the nursing home after all,
maybe I'll go to Danebo on Mississippi River Road
where my mother-in-law went when she was
eighty-one, where she fell in love
with a man she confided in me once
she thought she loved more than she'd ever
loved even papa, to whom she had been
married for almost fifty years,
and by whom she had borne five children.

Things I Didn't Know I Loved

– after reading Nazim Hikmet

Old cars, rusting away in farm groves,
as I drive down highway 212, old churches
Zion, Bethany, Emmanuel, Epiphany, Zoar,
yellow and green John Deer tractors
waiting on the outskirts of Danube, Hector, Renville.
Country western music after all the public radio
stations disappear, their themes of betrayal,
codependency, womanizing and alcoholism,
my friends waiting for me on their screen porch,
a little lunch, tuna hot dish and homemade dill pickles,
laid out on their round wooden table,
going to church the next day in town,
because Jody was playing in the bell choir,
all the girls and women in white gloves,
stroking their sweet bells with soft hammers,
during time for announcements,
Jennifer walking shyly up to the lectern
to announce: "Luther League will be going
bowling in Clarkfield tonight and out
afterwards for pizza and all you kids should
sign up after church even if you didn't before."

After our filling noon meal, vegetarian lasagna,
and tapioca pudding with ginger cookies,
resting and reading in the guest room,
finding Nazim Hikmet in the book shelf
above my bed, the poems of a Communist
who spent most of the 1930's and 40's
in Turkish jails because he was found guilty
of inciting military cadets to revolt –
loving his poems, so intimate and immediate,
not at all like the poems I'd expect from
a Communist, carrying his book downstairs
to read aloud to Howard and Jody before
I headed back to the city once again.

Garden Dream

I have pushed open the screen door
in a wide arc so it doesn't close too soon,
race to touch the cottonwood tree before
the door shuts, a childhood superstition.
I see a path right under the trellis
my father built leading to his garden,
a path I've never noticed before,
and I am intrigued, decide
to follow its dark packed dirt trail.

Beyond is the rich black soil my father
has already spaded this spring,
ready for the seeds to be sprinkled.
The path is narrow, but clear, well worn
by many feet, and I follow it, eager to find
where it leads, until I realize it is turning
into a tunnel. At first I am reluctant
to go further, fearing tunnels as I do,
but it is not totally dark in this tunnel,

some light glows from beyond, and I am
pleased to see that the path is widening,
that the tunnel is leading me into a space
filled with light, the kind of light a full moon
casts on the waters of Lake Superior in August.
The space grows larger until it stretches
out into infinity, filled with people
who have gathered to surprise me.
My mother is here, as she looked in

her confirmation picture, and my sister,
dressed in white for her 8th grade graduation,
which she didn't live to attend, and my brother
who died of pneumonia when he was only
three months old, now no longer a baby,
but wearing a new light-filled body. He
comes toward me at once, arms outstretched.
"We have been waiting for you," he says
embracing me. "Everyone is here. All is ready."

Still Writing, Still Painting

"Still writing?" he asks as I reach for a bunch of grapes at Lund's.
It's the distinguished poet whose workshops I've attended
and who once called me "a housewife poet," not to my face of course,
but it got back to me as these things often do.

What can I say now that he's caught me in a housewifely task?
His question hovers above the green and purple grapes
which I'm trying to decide whether to buy or not. I can never
remember if the boycott is off or on. "Yes, of course," I answer.
"I can't seem to stop doing it, even though the housework is piling up."

When I get home, I pick up a book I'd been reading about Gabriele Munter,
German artist who became the lover and soul mate of Kandinsky.
"I hold to Kandinsky. I give myself no worth next to him. He is a holy man."

But the holy man abandoned her after she'd devoted seventeen years
of her life to him, went back to Russia and took up with
a younger woman. Munter stopped painting for thirteen years,
then slowly started again, realizing her own work was holy too.

Her painting "Breakfast of the Birds" shows the back of a woman
sitting at a table looking out her window at a robin and chickadees
eating crumbs off snow-covered tree branches. On the white cloth
simple household objects, a tea pot, a sugar bowl, two plates,
bread and fruit – all surrounded by outlines of soft black paint.

I'm sitting at my table, notebook open, Pilot Razor Point pen poised,
gazing out my window at the snow-covered mountain ash in my courtyard,
thinking of Munter, still painting in her eighties, even as I am still writing
this poem in my seventies, right now, for you.